The Kingdom Of God In The Old Testament

Archibald Robertson

Kessinger Publishing's Rare Reprints

Thousands of Scarce and Hard-to-Find Books on These and other Subjects!

- Americana
- Ancient Mysteries
- Animals
- Anthropology
- Architecture
- Arts
- Astrology
- Bibliographies
- Biographies & Memoirs
- Body, Mind & Spirit
- Business & Investing
- Children & Young Adult
- Collectibles
- Comparative Religions
- Crafts & Hobbies
- Earth Sciences
- Education
- Ephemera
- Fiction
- Folklore
- Geography
- Health & Diet
- History
- Hobbies & Leisure
- Humor
- Illustrated Books
- Language & Culture
- Law
- Life Sciences

- Literature
- Medicine & Pharmacy
- Metaphysical
- Music
- Mystery & Crime
- Mythology
- Natural History
- Outdoor & Nature
- Philosophy
- Poetry
- Political Science
- Science
- Psychiatry & Psychology
- Reference
- Religion & Spiritualism
- Rhetoric
- Sacred Books
- Science Fiction
- Science & Technology
- Self-Help
- Social Sciences
- Symbolism
- Theatre & Drama
- Theology
- Travel & Explorations
- War & Military
- Women
- Yoga
- *Plus Much More!*

We kindly invite you to view our catalog list at:
http://www.kessinger.net

REGNUM DEI

LECTURE I

INTRODUCTORY. THE KINGDOM OF GOD IN THE OLD TESTAMENT

Thy kingdom is an everlasting kingdom, and thy dominion endureth throughout all generations.—Ps. cxlv. 13.

THE doubts and distractions of our age, and the questions at issue between the various systems which compete for the allegiance of the modern man, appear to turn ultimately upon the two kindred questions of the Government of the World and the purpose of Life. The two questions are not identical, for the former is speculative, and relates to the constitution of the world around us, while the other is strictly practical, and upon the answer to it depends the tone and colour of the individual life. But they are closely connected, for the practical question cannot receive even a practical answer without an implied assumption upon the wider issue. Common to both is the idea of purpose. Theoretically, if we can gain the conviction that purpose sways the forces of the universe and guides its history, it follows that man can only find the true end of his being in subordination to and in harmony with the Supreme Will which embraces nature and man in one. But practically, the process is reversed ; the more intense our sense of purpose in our individual life— the more lasting and comprehensive and satisfying the purpose which guides and sustains us as individuals, the more energetic becomes our hold upon the supreme truth of the Divine Government of the World, the deeper our homage in deed and thought to the absolutely Holy Will. The conviction of purpose in the individual life and the conviction of purpose in the universe, in short, act and react. The vigour of the one strengthens, the weakness of the one enfeebles, the other. Individual lives furnish exceptions to this general truth, but I speak of the tendency which asserts itself in the average and mass of human life.

To say this is to appeal to experience, the experience not only of the individual but still more of the human race. Believers have differed as to the theoretical cogency of the speculative proofs offered in support of the fundamental truths of God and the soul. I do not join in the tendency to disparage the proofs in question, on the contrary I believe them to be, so far as they go, indispensable and of great importance. But the mere fact that these proofs carry conviction, to equally sincere and religious minds, in very unequal degrees, must make us cautious of expecting too much from them. Moreover it is not as a matter of fact by means of them that we reach belief in God, or in ourselves as responsible beings. These priceless convictions come to us in all cases through those who possess them, and who have put them to the test of life. The religious experience of mankind is a fact unquestionable and unquestioned; the stream of religious conviction has flowed down to us from sources not all of which we can any longer trace, it has received tributaries, it has run in many channels and in varying degrees of depth and clearness and power. But wherever it has flowed it has kept alive that belief in the ultimate sovereignty of truth and right which is the central faith of all good men; it has upborne those who have faced with cheerfulness and courage the sharpest trials of life, and have raised and cheered the lives of their fellow-men. It is in the religious experience of mankind alone that the verification of religious conviction is to be found.[1]

That the Christian Religion, and its antecedent development, recorded in the Old Testament, constitute the centre and heart of the religious experience of mankind will not be disputed, even by those who regard all religious experience as founded upon illusion. Here, that which underlies all religion, though in many religions so mingled with heterogeneous matter as to be hard to discover, the simplest instinct of man's thirst for a living GOD,—finds its simplest expression, its simplest satisfaction. Here too we find prominence

---

[1] No two regions of thought could well be wider apart than that of the physicist reiterating his conviction, founded upon minute investigation of the building up of molecules and the behaviour of atoms, of "the rationality of all natural processes" (Dr. Larmor at the British Association, *Times* of Sept. 7, 1900), and that of Deborah (Judg. v. 11) rehearsing "the righteous acts of Jehovah toward his villages in Israel." The one is approaching God by intellectual steps, the other is drawing full-handed from religious experience. But both processes already meet in the prophecy of Amos as really, though not as analytically, as they do in the pages of St. Augustine himself.

given to the most elemental needs of our moral nature, both in its ideal loftiness and in its actual humiliation and weakness. Nowhere else are mythical and incongruous elements, fanaticisms and superstitions, so markedly absent, or, if present, so readily disengaged from the religion itself.

It is then worth while, or rather it is of the highest importance, to examine Christian experience with reference to the great twofold problem of life,—the purpose of God in guiding the affairs of man, and the supreme purpose—the *summum bonum*—which we are severally to set before us as the goal of our life.

Both aspects of the problem before us come, in the teaching of Christ, under the general conception of the Kingdom of GOD, the kingdom in which the consummation of the ages will find its final issue, and which we are each one of us first of all things to pray for and to seek, in the confidence that if that is gained, all subordinate good things will be added in GOD'S own time.

It is the purpose of these Lectures to contribute something, however small, toward the interpretation and thus to the vindication, of the supreme goal set before us by our Lord under the name of the Kingdom of GOD.

To interpret it adequately or worthily, even in its imperfect earthly manifestation, is a task wholly beyond individual power; the task is imposed upon the Society of all who bear Christ's name, and even so the interpretation must be progressive and subject to correction, and must remain imperfect in the end.

To promise a decisive and rounded-off conclusion would therefore condemn our attempt in advance. But what we can do is to interrogate Christian experience as disclosed in the history of the Christian Society. So far as the life and thought of that Society has been moulded by different conceptions of the Kingdom of GOD, those conceptions have been put to the test of experience, and as they have emerged confirmed or discredited, the result should enable us to distinguish between the more transitory and the more lasting elements in the Master Idea; and so we may learn to correct and purify our own ideals, and bring our working aims and convictions into closer correspondence with ultimate reality.

We must begin with the attempt to understand, so far as is possible, the meaning which our Lord himself gave to the Idea. This will occupy three Lectures; the present Lecture will sketch the Old Testament antecedents, the second, after placing in comparison the conceptions of the Kingdom of GOD entertained respectively by those whom our Lord found "waiting for" it, and by St. Paul the great Pharisee of the generation which had learned from Christ, will show how the points of agreement and difference alike presuppose the teaching of Christ as recorded in the synoptic Gospels. The third Lecture will complete this subject, and will consider the evidence derivable from the Fourth Gospel, the remaining Epistles, and the Apocalypse. The fourth Lecture will deal with the realistic eschatology of the primitive Church, as influenced in part by the Apocalypse, in part by other causes. This marks a very important, though transi-

tory, phase in the Christian conception of the Kingdom
of GOD. The fifth Lecture will aim at doing justice to
the influence of St. Augustine, as closing an epoch of
Christian thought on this subject, and as opening a
new epoch in which opposing conceptions, both rooted
in Augustine's thought, are destined to contend for the
mastery. In the sixth Lecture, the medieval papacy
will be treated as the attempt to give effect to one of
these alternative conceptions, viz. that of the Kingdom
of GOD as an omnipotent Church, an attempt in which
theory followed the lead of practice. The seventh
Lecture will describe the intellectual and moral break-
up of this system, and how, from being the ideal of
Christendom as a whole, it became theoretically
elaborated as that of a party in Christendom. Then,
after dealing briefly with the reassertion, at the Reformation, of one distinctively Augustinian conception
of the Church and with its consequences as affecting
the subject of our study, it will be endeavoured to
gather up the result of the whole enquiry, and to bring
its results to bear upon some problems which confront
the Christian in modern life. To do this will be the
object of the eighth and last Lecture.

II

One point must impress us at the outset of our
enquiry. Whatever difficulties may attend the attempt
to do justice to the fact in modern theology, there can
be no question that in our Lord's teaching the Kingdom
of GOD is the representative and all-embracing summary
of his distinctive mission. The Baptist came to an-

nounce that the Kingdom of GOD was at hand,[1] and when Jesus himself began to teach, what he taught is summed up in the same words,—"repent, for the kingdom of GOD has come near."[2] And it was not only the beginning of his teaching but the end as well. In the forty days before he was taken up, "he was seen of them, and was telling them the things concerning the kingdom of GOD."[3] Throughout, his message is "the good news of the kingdom,"[4]—the kingdom which comes with his coming,—to accept his gospel is to receive the Kingdom of GOD,[5] the first prayer he taught his disciples to address to their Father in heaven was "Thy kingdom come." Devout Israelites like Joseph of Arimathea and many others who pass before us in the gospel pages have this as the goal of their hopes, they are "looking for the kingdom of GOD."[6] It is to be the goal of Christian life and effort.[7] It sums up the preaching of the Apostles after the Lord's visible presence was withdrawn. Philip in Samaria, St. Paul at Ephesus and at Rome, preach and teach "concerning the kingdom of God."[8] "Descriptions" it has been truly said "of the characteristics of the kingdom, expositions of its laws, accounts of the way men were actually receiving it, forecasts of its future, make up the whole central portion of the synoptic narrative."[9]

But our Saviour did not begin by defining the

---

[1] Matt. iii. 2. [2] Matt. iv. 17, parallel with Mark i. 15.
[3] Acts i. 3. [4] Matt. iv. 23, xiii. 19.
[5] Matt. xii. 28; Mark x. 15; Luke xviii. 17.
[6] Mark xv. 43. [7] Matt. vi. 33; Luke xii. 31.
[8] Acts viii. 12, xix. 8, xx. 25, xxviii. 23, 31.
[9] Stanton, *The Jewish and the Christian Messiah*, p. 206.

Kingdom of GOD. He simply announced it. And this implies that his hearers, even those who were not, in the signal and pre-eminent sense, " waiting for the Kingdom of GOD," were prepared to attach some meaning to the phrase. Even the hostile Pharisees ask " when the kingdom of GOD is to come." [1]   Christ is not introducing an idea wholly new to his hearers, but is making use of one which already existed, and was exercising a spell over men's minds. What is told us of select individuals was true in a real, though a lower and less intimate sense of the nation as a whole. Christ found Israel as a nation looking for the Kingdom of GOD. This fact stands in the closest connexion with the national hope of a Messiah, an anointed king, who was to be raised up by GOD in the latter days to " restore again the kingdom to Israel," [2] to bring back national independence, and to revive all the splendour and national well-being which tradition associated with the kingdom of David. This hope varied doubtless in its character according to the spiritual capacities of those who cherished it; some thought more of the external and political, others of the religious blessings of which the Messiah-King was to be the bearer,—but it was universal, and in the more spiritual minds the idea of political deliverance was subordinated entirely to that of religious reformation and enlarged moral opportunity. Their hopes are expressed in the verse of the *Benedictus* : " That we being delivered from the hand of our enemies might serve him without fear, in holiness and right- eousness before him, all the days of our life." [3]   In

[1] Luke xvii. 20.   [2] Acts i. 6.   [3] Luke i. 74.

proclaiming that the Kingdom of GOD was at hand, Jesus Christ takes his stand upon the national hope of Israel. What then was the hope actually entertained by the nation? and how far did Christ really make it his own? This question can only be answered as we proceed; but meanwhile we may say thus much: Our Lord gradually untaught his Disciples the hope as they held it at the first, and taught it them again in a wholly transformed shape.

III

(a) Their hope had come down to them from the past. Like the Religion of Christ generally, this "exhaustive category" of Christ's teaching has its roots in the Old Testament. We shall indeed search the Old Testament in vain for the *phrase* "Kingdom of GOD" or "Kingdom of Heaven." It belongs to the vocabulary of the New Testament, not of the Old. But it has its antecedents and elements in the Old Testament; and for these we must now enquire. The most direct Old Testament source for the New Testament idea of the Kingdom of GOD is without doubt the book of Daniel, which in two passages—to be referred to more particularly later on—speaks of a kingdom to be set up by the Most High himself, a kingdom which his saints are to possess.[1] But the book of Daniel itself comes at the end of a long process of development or of divine schooling, in the

---

[1] Dan. ii. 44, vii. 14, 27. Dalman, *Worte Jesu,* p. 109, makes a distinction between the sense of βασιλεία in these two passages which I cannot wholly follow.

course of which Israel was led to frame its ideal of a Golden Age. Whereas other nations looked sadly back to their golden age over a long series of successive declensions, Israel alone "placed its golden age in the future." The religions of antiquity were pessimistic and despairing in their philosophy of history; the religion of Israel was a religion of hope. From early times the germ of this phenomenon may be detected in the consciousness of a relation of the people to its GOD unlike anything that could be found in any other people—a relation which carried with it a peculiar consecration and an exceptional destiny. Their tradition of the great deliverance from Egypt told how Moses had promised them in Jehovah's name that if they would obey his voice they would be "a peculiar treasure unto me above all people—for all the earth is mine:—and ye shall be unto me a kingdom of priests and an holy nation."[1] The passage is regarded by critics as Deuteronomic in style and date, *i.e.* as tinged with the influence of the later prophets; but in substance the idea expressed is as old as any prophecy of which we know. The prophecies of Balaam describe how "It is a people that dwell alone, and shall not be reckoned among the nations"[2]—Israel was thought of, at any rate by its religious leaders, as marked off from other nations,—governed by no human king—over whom "Jehovah shall reign for ever and ever"[3]— Gideon refuses the throne for this reason: "I will not rule over you, neither shall my son rule over you: Jehovah shall rule over you."[4] When the people

---

[1] Ex. xix. 5, 6.   [2] Num. xxiii. 9.
[3] Ex. xv. 18.   [4] Judg. viii. 23.

demand a king, it is not Samuel, but Jehovah himself, whom they are deposing, "they have not rejected thee, but they have rejected me that I should not be king over them." [1] "When ye saw that Nahash king of the children of Ammon came against you, ye said unto me, Nay, but a king shall reign over us; when Jehovah your God was your king." [2] This protest means that Israel is, as a nation, a kingdom of GOD; the practical demand involved is for the surrender of the nation's self to the rule and guidance of their God, Jehovah, who had by his mighty works made himself known to them as their deliverer, "I am Jehovah thy God who brought thee up out of the land of Egypt,—thou shalt have none other god but me." [3] To assign a time for the origin of this ideal is I think not possible; in germ it appears coeval with the beginnings of the distinctive nationality and religion of Israel. But we may ask with more prospect of a definite result when and how this ideal became energetically formulated, and by what steps it led to the expectation of a future Kingdom of GOD.

Israel comes before us in its earliest scarcely dateable records as a group of tribes, very loosely organised, but able, when great occasions arose, to co-operate

---

[1] 1 Sam. viii. 7.   [2] 1 Sam. xii. 12.

[3] Ex. xx. 2, and often. What is contended is not that other peoples of antiquity, and Israel's nearest neighbours (Moab as in Mesha's Stone) were not theocratic, but that the moral character of Jehovah, and the moral link between him and his people, were conceived by the earliest religious teachers of the Israelites in a way to which the religion of other peoples does not furnish a parallel. That the reciprocal relation between Jehovah and Israel is *moral* is involved in germ in the idea of Covenant. (See W. Robertson Smith, *Prophets of Israel*, chap. ii. [1st ed.]; Ritschl, *Unterricht*, § 7, and Dr. Davidson's art. "Covenant" in Hastings' *Dict. of the Bible*.

more or less completely as a whole.   And when they
do so, the bond of union between the tribes is Jehovah.
Defaulters are traitors to him.   " Curse ye Meroz, said
the angel of Jehovah, curse ye bitterly the inhabitants
thereof; because they came not to the help of Jehovah
—to the help of Jehovah against the mighty." [1]   The
wars of Israel are recorded as " the wars of Jehovah "; [2]
the cause of the nation is his cause; scandalous offences
are sins against the collective national conscience—
" folly in Israel."

But we do not trace in the earliest history any such
profound sense of the unfitness of the people Israel to
be the vehicle of a spiritual idea as to lead them to
lean upon *the future* for the realisation of the golden
age of a true kingdom of GOD.

This deepening of the national conscience was the
work of the nation's experience under the Monarchy.
The Monarchy is presented to us in tradition under
two contrasted but really complementary aspects.

(1) On the one hand the religious conservatism of
the people, and the religious idealism of their teachers,
alike resented the centralisation of political power.
The language of Samuel already quoted gives strong
expression to this resentment.   The warning of
Deuteronomy [3] as to the evils which would attend the
establishment of a kingdom are in harmony with those
of Samuel, [4] and both find their verification in the reign
of King Solomon. [5]   There are many indications that

---

[1] Judg. v. 23.   [2] Num. xxi. 14.
[3] Deut. xvii. 14.   [4] 1 Sam. viii. 10–18.
[5] In Deut. the warnings are directed against (1) multiplication of horses,
(2) intercourse with Egypt, (3) multiplication of wives, (4) multiplication
of silver and gold, (5) overweening pride.   Samuel assumes (1) (4) and (5)

the monarchy was established before the nation was politically ripe for it—the reign of David over Judah was for some years confronted with the allegiance of Israel to Ishbosheth; the details of Absalom's revolt show that the ascendency which David succeeded in establishing over Israel was purely personal, and maintained itself in spite of a deep cleavage between the Northern and the Southern portions of the kingdom.[1] The census of the whole nation was an innovation amounting, in the eyes even of Joab, to sacrilege, and when it was carried out Judah and Israel were still treated as separate units. Solomon's reorganisation of the country for the purpose of taxation [2] looks [3] like an attempt to supersede the tribal organisation by one conceived on fiscal and political lines, centralised round Judah. The principal fiscal officer [4] appointed by Solomon was stoned as soon as the great king was dead—and even when he was at the height of his

and adds (6) forced labour, a standing army (practically identifiable with (1), and heavy taxation in kind (cf. (4)), coupled with (7) confiscations of real property (v. 14). All these apply to Solomon except (7) of which there is no direct evidence, and (6) which also seems doubtful (comp. 1 Kings ix. 22 with xii. 4, etc.).

[1] 2 Sam. xix. 41.   [2] 1 Kings iv. 7 sqq.

[3] Four tribes are ignored: Simeon, Dan, Zebulon, and Reuben—and of course Levi. Judah is not provided for, excepting that the Philistine border is administered as two departments. Four tribes are left as departments: Benjamin, Naphthali, Ephraim (i.e. its hill country), and Asher. The latter receives an added district. Probably Western Manasseh may be added, or at least that part which included the plain of Sharon (Naphath-Dor). Eastern Manasseh, Gad, and Issachar are curiously subdivided. The N. division of Issachar has the tribal name, but may have included part of Zebulon. The two Eastern tribes form three departments not easy to delimit. The outlying and especially the richer districts seem to receive careful reorganisation; the whole plan suggests that Judah is the only tribe whose allegiance can be taken for granted.

[4] Adoniram (or Adoram), 1 Kings iv. 6, xii. 18.

power, the voice of prophecy, in the memorable scene between Ahijah and Jeroboam, had doomed the precarious fabric of a united Israel to an early fall. Ahijah, it is true, bases his message upon the personal sin of Solomon, not upon any condemnation of monarchy as such. He may not, for all we know, have shared the feelings of Samuel on that subject. But Samuel's influence was too great to die with him, and of his view of the monarchy no doubt is permitted to us: he looked upon it as an apostasy from the nation's religious ideal.

(2) But the Monarchy has another and widely different aspect in religious tradition. On purely utilitarian grounds, indeed, the advantages of a central authority were obvious and tangible. Men looked back with relief from the times of monarchy, with all its faults, upon the anarchy which had preceded it. "In those days there was no king in Israel: every man did that which was right in his own eyes."[1] But this was only a small part of the truth. The reign, the achievements, and the personality of David formed the nucleus of an ideal which struck deep and lasting root in popular feeling. Amid their later vicissitudes, the Hebrews forgot the many failures of David's reign in comparison with its unquestionable splendours. Under David the Hebrew kingdom had been—for its opportunities—great and successful, its foreign wars untarnished by defeat, its king reigning in closest loyalty to Jehovah, the home life of the people protected from invasion, but not interfered with by the state. Oriental peoples are as a rule little appreciative

[1] Judg. xvii. 6, xviii. 1, xxi. 25.

of civil organisation ; they will *respect* only a strong
ruler ; but they will *love* a monarch who is in sympathy
with their character. Like the Persians who remem-
bered Cyrus as a Father,[1] Cambyses as a master,
Darius as a tradesman, the Hebrews, apparently in
Israel and Judah alike, cherished the memory of David
as the symbol of a glorious past, and the highest
embodiment of their hopes for a happier future. Even
Amos, whose mission is in Northern Israel, and Hosea,
a north-Israelite by birth and sentiment, equally with
Micah the prophet of the Judean peasantry, contrast-
ing later kings and later reigns with the traditional
glories of David, associate the future resurrection of
national life with a new David and a new national
unity under a regenerated dynasty of David's line.[2]

Secondly, the monarchy did in a very real sense
centralise the national conscience ; this allowed the
contrast between the ideal and the actual to come to
a head, and thus the way was prepared for the growth
of a more definite hope of an age to come. This
contrast was heightened by the manifest and increasing
decay of social life, and the divorce of religion from
conduct, both of which evils are lashed by Amos and
Isaiah, and by that assimilation of the religion of
Jehovah to local worships which is denounced by

---

[1] Herod. III. lxxxix. : ὅτι ἤπιός τε καὶ ἀγαθά σφι πάντα ἐμηχανήσατο.
The contrasted reference is to Darius' careful organisation of the finances
of his empire.

[2] I take the passages in question as they stand, though fully aware that
Professor Sayce (*Higher Criticism and Mon.*, chaps. ix. and x.) and others
hold that Amos and Hosea bear marks of Judean editing ; the identifica-
tion of these marks appears somewhat subjective, and I cannot follow Professor Charles (*Eschatology*, p. 83) in extending the principle to most of the
Messianic passages in the four earliest prophetical books.

Hosea. These corruptions were linked, in the prophetic survey of the times, with the overhanging peril of Assyria, which the prophets interpreted as the scourge which was to purify the life of Israel and bring about the establishment of a regenerated kingdom.

From the death of Solomon down to that of Uzziah—or the contemporary close of the reign of Jeroboam II.—the name " Israel " belongs specially to the northern kingdom.[1] The main volume of national life, the chief vicissitudes of religious history, the great prophetic personalities, and the very important though somewhat obscure institutions of prophetic fraternities, from which the great and individually inspired prophets stand out like peaks from a range of lower heights, all are found in the kingdom of Israel, and lend undying interest to its records. With the death of Uzziah and the call of Isaiah we find Israel already hastening to political effacement and Judah fully ripe to continue the development for a time. About this time we trace the earliest form of eschatological hope, the germ from which both the definite expectation of a personal Messiah-king and that of a kingdom of GOD derive their origin—viz. the hope of a restored and purified Israel. The great pre-canonical prophets, indeed, were concerned with the present rather than with the future. Elijah, no doubt, when he despairs of Israel as it is, is rebuked [2] by the reminder of the seven thousand who have not bowed the knee to Baal;—and this conception of a faithful minority,

[1] Reference may be permitted to an article by the present writer which aims at doing justice to the Biblical estimate of Northern Israel (*The Thinker*, Jan. 1895).

[2] 1 Kings xix. 14-18.

who were to form the nucleus of a regenerated people,
was destined to become fruitful in the hands of later prophets.   But his main mission, and that of Elisha also,
was different, namely to be "very jealous" for the Lord of
Hosts—to vindicate the *exclusive sovereignty* of Jehovah
over Israel.   Both Elijah and Elisha exemplify the
growing prophetic consciousness that Israel is far below
the ideal of a "people of Jehovah."   But Elisha's direct
mission is simply to supersede a sinful dynasty; and he
lives long enough to see how little such a remedy can
really effect.

With Amos and Hosea begins a new prophetic
epoch; not merely the beginning of written prophecy,
although this implies much, but the opening out of a
wider outlook upon the forces which were moulding the
future of the world, and a longer vista of time—an outlook upon a future of which we do yet see to the end.
The contemporaries of Amos had the expectation of a
"day of the Lord"—they hoped for some decisive
intervention by Jehovah in favour of his people which
would relieve the anxieties which were crowding round
them, and proclaim Jehovah and his people Israel
victorious over their foes.   To these hopes Amos sternly
gives the lie.   The day of Jehovah would come indeed,
but not such a day as they expected.   "Woe unto you
that desire the day of the LORD.   Wherefore would ye
have Jehovah's day : shall not Jehovah's day be dark-
ness and not light—even very dark and no brightness
in it ? "   Jehovah has indeed a special care for Israel,
but the first result of this will be sharp and speedy
vengeance upon their sins.   "You only have I known
of all the families of the earth—therefore I will punish

you for your iniquities." [1]   And Hosea, though he
dwells upon the unquenchable love of Jehovah for Israel,
holds out no hope of escape from the terrible collapse
of the nation which the immediate future is to bring.
Both prophets however look for restoration, to follow,
and to be effected by, the furnace of affliction, and both
associate the regeneration of the people with a revival
of the monarchy of David.   Here then we have the
contrast between the ideal and the actual formulated
with all possible clearness, and while the actual present
is painted with ruthless severity, the ideal is assured in
the future.   But it is in Isaiah that this new germ of
prophecy is ripened to a head.   His denunciation of the
present is most marked and unsparing in the prophecies
which immediately follow his call " in the year that
King Uzziah died,"[2] *i.e.* in the early days of Ahaz. " How
long ? " is the keynote of these earlier utterances.   Then
under Ahaz comes the combination of denunciation and
promise, when special prominence is given to the thought
of a king under whom the divine guidance of Israel shall
once more be the ruling reality of the nation's life.
Immanuel will appear, and that very shortly, and the
land of Israel is his destined kingdom.   Meanwhile,
Isaiah has collected round him a band of disciples, who
will, so it would seem, form a nucleus for the remnant
that shall escape the overflowing scourge and constitute
the beginnings of a new and worthier people of Jehovah.
Under Hezekiah the promise is more clearly formulated.
The personality of the Messiah-king is now less pro-

[1] Amos v. 18-20, iii. 2.   See Charles, *Eschatology*, pp. 82, 84 sqq.
[2] It is impossible to assign any considerable time for an independent
reign of Jotham.

minent, but the regenerate kingdom fills the prophet's imagination.[1]   It is linked on with the actual Israel by the remnant that will be spared when the scourge of Jehovah's anger has passed over the land: but although the realisation of the blessed future will be in and for Israel, the whole world will share in it.   The regenerate kingdom will be a channel of blessing to all mankind; even Assyria and Egypt, the two signal representatives of the hostile world-empire, will be numbered with Israel as God's people and the work of his hands.[2]

(*b*) The next period of prophecy, under Josiah and his sons, coincides with the discovery of Deuteronomy, in which book Moses is interpreted to the people by the prophets—the ancient law passing, through the medium of prophecy, into the national consciousness.   As a result, the faithful minority become more sharply defined; and at the same time their world-wide mission is again emphasised.   " Seek ye Jehovah, all ye meek of the earth—it may be ye shall be hid in the day of Jehovah's anger."   " For I will turn to the peoples a pure language, that they may all call upon the name of Jehovah, to serve him with one consent."   " But I will leave in the midst of them an afflicted and poor people, and they shall trust in the name of Jehovah."[3]   Here we very nearly reach the universalism of the 87th

---

[1] Isa. xxxiii.

[2] Isa. xix. 16–25. The universalism of this passage is a splendid paradox in the mouth of a contemporary of Hezekiah. But to put the passage far later than the Assyrian period (Charles, p. 113) is surely a more startling historical paradox. Micah, the prophet of the Judean peasantry, has in common with Isaiah the hope of a renewed purity of national life, and of a Davidic prince. But unlike Isaiah, he demands the destruction of the sinful capital (iii. 12, iv. 10, i. 5). In this, he anticipates Jeremiah.

[3] Zeph. ii. 3, iii. 9, 12. For another side to Zephaniah, see Charles, p. 98.

Psalm, in which the thought of Isa. xix. is carried
to its highest development—

> I will make mention of Rahab and Babylon as among them
> that know me.
> Behold Philistia, and Tyre, with Ethiopia ;
> This one was born there.
> Yea of Zion shall it be said, This one and that one was born
> in her.
> The LORD shall count, when he writeth up the peoples,
> This one was born there.

To this period, again, belongs the first formulation of
the underlying principle of universalism [1] in the famous
verse of Habakkuk, which furnished St. Paul with the
text for his Epistle to the Romans, " The just shall live
by his faith." [2] And even more explicit is the superb
passage of Jeremiah, [3] " Behold the days come, saith
Jehovah, that I will make a new covenant with the house
of Israel . . . but this is the covenant that I will make
with the house of Israel after these days, saith Jehovah :
I will put my law in their inward parts and in their hearts
will I write it ; and I will be their GOD and they shall
be my people : and they shall teach no more every one
his neighbour, and every one his brother saying know
Jehovah: for they shall all know me from the least of them
unto the greatest of them, saith Jehovah ; for I will forgive
their iniquity, and their sin will I remember no more."
The great passage to be thoroughly appreciated must
be read with its whole context. [4] The entire section is the

---

[1] By universalism, in this connexion, is meant the principle of a universal
religion, in which there is no difference before GOD between "Jew and
Greek " (Gal. iii. 28, etc.).

[2] Hab. ii. 4. By " faith" here is meant not merely "integrity " but
"trust in God." See Riehm, A T. Theol. § 74. 4.

[3] Jer. xxxi. 31 sqq.   [4] Jer. xxx., xxxi.

ripest fruit of the prophetic picture of a perfect kingdom in which GOD himself is King. In one verse[1] Jeremiah recalls Hosea's prophecy of a Davidic monarchy,[2] but throughout the passage as a whole it is the direct reign of GOD in the hearts and lives of his people that is really in contemplation. It may be questioned whether the Christian conception of a kingdom of GOD upon earth has ever, even at its highest, done more than touch the height here attained. Certainly it has often done less.

Ezekiel in one passage[3] partially reproduces the thought of Jeremiah. Generally speaking, however, universalism, though present, is not prominent, in Ezekiel. Certainly in the earlier part of his prophecy (i.–xxiv.) he shows that the existing kingdom and priest-hood[4] are not to be identified with the promised king-dom. The growth of the tender shoot to a goodly cedar, in whose shadow shall dwell " fowl of every wing,"[5] reminds us of the mustard seed of the Gospels ; and the hope of restoration is expressly extended even to the most profligate of heathen cities.[6]

In the second and reconstructive part (xxxiii.–end) we have the wonderful anticipation[7] of the Parable of the Good Shepherd, the stony heart replaced by hearts of flesh,[8] and above all the great prophecy of the bones,[9] which—once again in the spirit of Hosea—promises resurrection to Israel and Judah equally under the

[1] Jer. xxx. 9.   [2] See Briggs, *Messianic Prophecy*, p. 255 sqq.
[3] Ezek. xi. 16-20.   [4] xxi. 26, 27.
[5] xvii. 22-24. I venture to dissent from Professor Charles' view (p. 106, note) that "all fowl of every wing " cannot refer to the Gentiles.
[6] xvii. 53.   [7] xxxiv. 11-31.
[8] xxxvi. 25-35, cf. xi. 16-20.   [9] xxxvii. 1-24.

monarchy of David. This prophecy certainly extends far beyond mere restoration from exile ; it is a *spiritual* restoration above all that is promised. And the great picture of a restored and reorganised Jewish Church-People culminates in the waters of life, which are to revive even the Dead Sea,[1] as those of Paradise watered the whole earth.

We see then the seed of universalism steadily unfolding and striking root at the beginning of the Exile. And if we are to yield to the evidence which brings down to the period of exile large portions of our present book of Isaiah, the continuity of development is illustrated by them in a remarkable way. National regeneration is to follow upon the overthrow of Babylon. The faithfulness of Jehovah will bring into being a renewed Israel who will inherit the nations. The servant of Jehovah is not only to embody the ideal character which is to emerge from the long discipline of the nation, but he is also to be a light to the Gentiles.[2] And all culminates in a new Palestine, a very heaven on earth,[3] and in a renewal of the Heavens and Earth themselves.[4] Here we have for the first time the germ of a purely eschatological conception of the kingdom, eschatological in the sense of transcending altogether the conditions of earthly existence, and reserved for a future world. The eschatology of the Prophets is, so far, almost wholly concerned with the life of the nation, and with what shall befall it in the last days. But the thought upon which we have just touched opens the

---

[1] Ezek. xlvii. 12, cf. xvii. 53.
[2] Isa. xlix. 14–23, li. 1–8, liv. 1 sqq., lvi. 6, 7, lx.   [3] Isa. xxxv.
[4] lxv. 17 sqq. See Charles, *Eschatology*, p. 122 sqq.

way to a fusion of the eschatology of the nation—the distinctive theme of prophecy—with the eschatology of the individual, which had hitherto played no part in the accredited religious training of GOD's people, though we can trace in popular belief and custom,[1] and occasionally in the language of prophets themselves, the existence of some belief at any rate in a personal existence continued after death. What we have specially to take note of at this period,—that of the Exile, from Jeremiah to Haggai,—is a conception of a resurrection from death as the privilege of the righteous individual—the direct germ of the distinctively Christian doctrine of a resurrection from the dead. The comparison is instructive between the resurrection-language of Hosea [2] and that of the 26th chapter of Isaiah [3] which in some ways recalls it. In Hosea the resurrection is clearly and definitely that of the nation. In the later passage the thought of individual resurrection begins to make its presence felt, though the predominant thought is still — as in the great prophecy of Ezekiel—that of corporate revival.

On the whole, we seem to detect a transition in its beginnings. We may say that the downfall of the Jewish State deepened and widened the hopes of the Nation by preparing the transition to the idea of a kingdom of GOD in a new life, and *therefore* based upon the resurrection of at any rate the righteous dead. This has as its necessary correlative an increased concentration of interest upon individual righteousness and holiness, individual religion ; and this again centres

---

[1] See Charles, *Eschatology*, pp. 56, 62, 69–76, 125.

[2] Hos. vi. 2, xiii. 14.

[3] Isa. xxvi. 19 and context, see Charles, p. 126 sq.

attention upon the inward and spiritual state as the ground of righteousness in God's sight.

We have noticed the characteristic declaration of this everlasting truth by Habakkuk as well as Jeremiah, Ezekiel and the rest. The kingdom to which these later prophets look forward is, accordingly, Jewish in its origin, but for the benefit of all mankind; Zechariah (if the chapters in question belong approximately to this period) insists [1] upon the religious attraction which will draw all the world to Jerusalem,[2] Haggai[3] sees them pouring all their treasures into the house of Jehovah, and fierce as is the vengeance which Joel denounces upon those who have enslaved and sold the children of Jerusalem, there is no need to interpret more narrowly than did the Apostles his prophecy that the LORD in time to come would pour out his Spirit "upon *all* flesh," and that "whosoever shall call on the name of the LORD shall be saved."[4]

---

[1] Zech. viii. 23, xiv. 16. On the current view of the dates, see Charles, pp. 117, 121.

[2] The "Apocalypse" of Zechariah xii. 1–9, xiv. has features in common with Zephaniah (Charles, 98), Ezekiel xlvii. 1–12 (see Charles, 106), and with Joel iv. 18 (Charles, 118). See also Isa. xxxiv., xxxv. It represents a final capture of Jerusalem by the heathen, leading to a signal Theophanic Deliverance, followed by the gathering in of the Nations round a nucleus of believing Israelites. This final struggle has a long sequel in the history of Apocalyptic vision. See Charles, pp. 122 (Daniel), 177 (Sibyl), 191 (Enoch *Ethiop.*), 247 (Jubiles), 288 (4 Esdras), 348 sq., 381. "The doctrine of a final overthrow of living enemies—enemies of Israel according to Jewish belief, enemies of GOD and his true kingdom according to the more spiritual view of Christians—retained its place among the Last Things . . . even when the doctrine of a universal eternal judgment upon every human being, dead as well as living, was added" (see Stanton, *The Jewish and the Christian Messiah*, pp. 136 sq., 304–310).

[3] Hag. ii. 6–9.

[4] Joel ii. 32. Charles, p. 119, mainly on the ground of iii. 2 sqq., which I regard as inconclusive, insists upon a "particularist" sense of this verse.

The Exile then, or rather the experiences of the people which led to it, accompanied it, and followed it, prepared the faithful Israelites for the thought of (1) a kingdom of GOD within them, (2) a kingdom of GOD spiritual and world-wide, and (3) a kingdom of God in a life to come.

(c) The subsequent history gives increased definiteness and force to this hope, but at the same time forces it into a somewhat narrower channel. The ideal of the Exile seems at first sight to lose something of the sanguine sympathy and world-wide range of its early promise.

The hope of the Prophets is in fact attuned by Daniel to the faith of an oppressed people, struggling for independence, and conscious that the institutions distinctive of their religion are at stake in the struggle. Whether Daniel wrote under the present stress of the Maccabean struggle, or foresaw it in the minuteness of detail of which chap. xi. is the witness, that chapter is at any rate enough to show the situation to which the book is closely addressed. Faced with the alternative of apostasy or annhilation, the pious Israelite is to learn that stedfast loyalty to his GOD will come out triumphant however the odds to which it is opposed. This, the common creed of prophecy, Daniel enforces by a new method,—new, that is, in its literary vehicle, but with its roots in the prophetic past. Daniel stands first in the great series of Apocalypses. Viewed as they formerly were from a distance, the visions of Daniel and of St. John towered aloft into the light of heaven, two solitary mountain peaks connecting heaven and earth. We have now been brought by the study of comparative material to a nearer point of view; we see that the giant masses are connected and surrounded by a long series of lesser heights; Apocalypses of Moses, of Eldad and Medad, of Elijah and Isaiah, of Enoch and Abraham, of the XII Patriarchs, of Ezra and Baruch, and of Peter. Apocalypse is a type of literature as distinctive of Judaism as the drama is distinctive of the Greeks, and there are characteristics which are common to the whole Apocalyptic series. But it remains as true as formerly that in the whole range two peaks alone catch the sunlight of Inspiration.

Apocalypse furnished the Jew with a philosophy of history in relation to religion and life. This had in a measure been the work of prophecy and of certain other classes of Hagiographa. But Apocalypse addressed itself directly and comprehensively to the history of the world, with the history of the Chosen People as its centre, viewed in the light of the ultimate purpose of GOD, and the final consummation of his Kingdom.

In the book of Daniel three points claim our special attention. First the history of the world is reviewed twice over (chaps. ii., vii.); it culminates in a hostile power, apparently centred in an individual king (vii. 8, viii. 9, 21, xi., all apparently identical in reference), which is to be overthrown by a divine, a perfect and an eternal kingdom, reigned over by " one like unto a Son of Man," *i.e.* by the people of the saints of the Most High.[1] Secondly, this kingdom is inaugurated by judgment—a judgment with books[2] and penal fire for the enemies.[3]

---

[1] Dan. vii. 13.　On the meaning of this see Driver, *Daniel*, p. 108.
[2] Dan. vii. 10, cf. xii. 2.
[3] Dan. vi. 11, cf. Isa. lxvi. fin.; Charles, pp. 132, 181.

The resurrection which ushers in the judgment is still not conceived as universal; but it is individual, and it includes bad as well as good. Thirdly, the intensity and definiteness of the whole is undoubtedly gained at the expense of the older prophetic universalism. The nationalism of Daniel is intense. But it is tempered by deep national contrition (ix. 3–19); and the seer has learned, before St. Paul was there to teach him, that " not all are Israel " who are of Israel's seed.[1] Those only who are written in the book are delivered, and not all endure to the end. Still, we certainly miss here the hope held out by the prophets for all mankind. True, there is nothing to forbid proselytism, but even that has no special mention, still less anything beyond it. But though this is so, the reign of the Son of Man is to include all mankind : " that all people and nations and language should serve him." The possession of the kingdom is, indeed, reserved to the saints,—*i.e.* to those against whom the tyrant has waged war,[2]—but it will—under conditions not defined—include all the world. There are two factors in the idea of the Messianic kingdom in the maturity of Jewish prophecy,—the idea of universal dominion, and the idea of a universal conversion of mankind to the worship of Jehovah—the political and the purely religious conception of the Divine kingdom on earth. The two are not mutually exclusive, but are two alternative aspects of one and the

---

[1] Dan. xii. 12, 1 sqq.

[2] Dan. vii. 18, 21, 22. Charles says, somewhat curtly, " There is no Messiah." This would imply, what is not the case, that a Messiah is not only not named, but excluded. And Enoch (B.C. 90, see Charles, p. 214 sq., and Driver, *l.c.*) already understands the "Son of Man" in Dan. as the Messiah.

same general expectation. In Daniel it must be said that the thought of universal dominion predominates over the other. The book contemplates conversion by means of dominion rather than dominion by means of conversion. And this gives the keynote for the hope of the Kingdom of GOD as we see it in possession of men's minds at the coming of Christ. The circumstances of the times—of the last two centuries before Christ, made dependence upon a heathen power more than ever intolerable to the Jews. The Pharisees, who were above all else religious loyalists, became the spiritual leaders of the people. And in foreign dominion the Pharisees saw a direct menace against the purity of the national religion. Only, in the higher minds, the aspiration for political independence was strictly subordinated to that for religious purity. To be rid of hostile domination was a means, not an end in itself. The aim was at bottom spiritual—the free and unhampered service of GOD: "That we, being delivered from our enemies, might serve him without fear: in holiness and righteousness before him, all the days of our life."

This was the hope that had sustained the sons of Matthias and their followers in their devoted, and on the whole successful, struggle against Greek domination and influence in the second century before Christ; and the same hope, kept alive by the zeal of the Pharisees, sustained the faith of the people through the depressing days of Roman and Herodian power.

The purity of motive which at first marks out the family of the Maccabees begins indeed from a very early date to suffer from earthly alloy. The last surviving brother, Simeon, united the office of High Priest with the functions, though not with the express title, of king.[1]   Under him priesthood practically merges in royalty.   The indirect result is to increase the importance of the Scribe and the synagogue as factors in popular religion, at the expense of the temple and the priest.   Simeon's son, Hyrcanus the first, destroyed the Temple of Gerizim and vainly endeavoured to force the Samaritans into ecclesiastical conformity.   With the Edomites he was more successful.   Political aims and methods more and more displace the spirit in which the family had first attained their power.   Judas Aristobulus I., the eldest son of Hyrcanus, formally assumed the style and title of king; his brother, Alexander Jannaeus,[2] gradually relapsed into a mere head of the Sadducees.   Involved in civil war and bloodshed, he left his widow to break with the Sadducees and rule justly during the minority of their sons.   The rivalries of these sons, the weak devotee Hyrcanus II. and the more spirited Aristobulus, the intervention of Pompey, the bloody siege and capture of Jerusalem, and the profanation of the Temple, need not be recalled at length.   As a result, Hyrcanus was left as High Priest but not as king.   His granddaughter and sole surviving representative, the unfortunate Mariamne, married the son of his Edomite major-domo Antipater, and by the favour of Mark Antony the monarchy founded upon the purest movement of intense religious zeal passed into the hands of Herod the Great.

The Maccabean house had in fact followed up self-sacrifice by self-aggrandisement; they began as

---

[1] From his reign date the first known Jewish coins (B.C. 139).

[2] B.C. 106-79.

defenders of a purely spiritual cause, but ended by usurping both the high-priesthood and the throne. In both ways they violated the principle of legitimate succession which had become so sacred in Jewish eyes; they set it aside not for any more spiritual principle, but merely as political opportunists. No wonder then that this relapse from their first purity cost them the whole-hearted support of the religious purists who had at first carried them to power. No consistent Pharisee could wholly accept a High Priest who did not represent the legitimate line of Aaron, or tolerate, as an embodiment of his hope of the Messianic kingdom, a king who had no pretence to descent from David. That some did not share this attitude of strict protest, and rallied to the *de facto* dynasty, was a matter of course. Such is always apt to be the case, and the tendency accounts for the existence in gospel times of the party of Herodians. But it is not in such quarters that we must look for the hope of the Kingdom of GOD to which our Lord made his first appeal. The deeper religious feeling to which I have just referred found expression, in the very generation which ushered in the Christian era, in the Psalms of Solomon of which I will speak in the next Lecture.

IV

Meanwhile, let us briefly gather up the results of our survey of the Messianic expectation in its growth and modification to the close of O.T. times. The idea of the Kingdom of GOD took shape at first as a virtual philosophy of history, and a philosophy of history presupposes a philosophy of life and existence. In other words, faith in GOD himself lies behind the idea of his purpose for his rational creation—*i.e.* behind the idea of a kingdom of GOD. A GOD who is not supreme over nature can have no effective purpose for beings whose bodily constitution and surroundings are at the mercy of nature's forces. Now whatever re-arrangements may be necessary in the order of the documents of the O.T., or in the inferred order of religious development, it must, I think, be allowed that the idea of GOD presented to us in the Old Testament is distinctive from the first in this very respect. Anthropomorphic and anthropopathic language and thought there is,—limitations from which the mind, especially the popular mind, was only gradually cleared. That the personal name [1] of the national deity of one small nation, coupled with the early experiences in which that nation saw the arm of their national God, should have supplied the real and absolute point of contact between the human race and the Personal Existence, which underlies the boundless seen and unseen universe, and guides its every movement from the greatest to the least, is a thing hard at first sight to conceive. But when we see the fact in all its context, and realise that *there* is the beginning of every advance that religion has made in the world, the original starting-point of all Christian prayers and hopes and efforts, the fountain-head of all that is

---

[1] Justin Martyr, resting upon the LXX rendering κύριοσ for מהי, makes it a proof of the purity of O.T. religion that, unlike heathen deities, the God of Israel lacked a personal name (θεὸν ὄνομα, *Apol.* 1. x., cf. *Cohort. ad Graec.* xxi.). This of course cannot now be maintained, but the essential difference, as stated in the text, remains.

noblest in thought, word and action around us to-day,
he would indeed be rash who should dismiss it as in-
credible.　If the sequel has been on such a momentous
scale, we cannot doubt that some consciousness of what
it meant was present in the minds that first received
the tender seed of divine revelation.　Men set out on
the first stages of their journey toward the hope of
GOD'S kingdom with a belief, implicit if not formally
expressed, that the GOD in whom they trusted was
able to perform all that he promised.　The Israelites,
then, from time immemorial, thought of their God in a
way that implied a lofty and exclusive moral allegiance,
—their earliest political unity was that of a kingdom of
GOD.　And then by a series of national experiences
which we are partly able to trace in detail, and into
which the institution of monarchy and the work of the
prophets entered as leading factors, they were led to
realise how little their actual condition corresponded
with this great idea, and to look for a time to come
when the ideal would be realised in the future, as it
had never been in the past, of a righteous people
reigned over by the GOD of all the universe.　This
future was conceived in the form of a perfect Kingdom,
and its realisation hung upon the coming of a King in
whose person the reign of GOD should find its final and
absolute expression.　In the great prophets who saw
and followed the downfall of the Monarchy, this hope
reached its most spiritual conception, and embodied a
principle which left no room for the distinctive privilege
of the Jew, but included all nations on a common basis
of spiritual regeneration.　Later on, in response to a
crisis which called for concentrated and warlike action,

this world-wide range of sympathy was somewhat narrowed, and the kingdom was figured in terms more distinctively Jewish. But the faith itself was the more intense and keen, and after burning now more dimly, now again brighter in the century and a half which preceded the birth of Christ, now once more popular expectation watched with feverish anxiety for the Person of the predestined King. It has been said of late, by one whose moral earnestness has left its mark upon this place, that the Messianic hope is a Jewish dream, the creation of national vanity, and without importance or interest to the modern mind.[1] As long as the best men and women, the very salt of human society, pray Thy kingdom come,—as long as the command, to seek first the Kingdom of GOD and his Righteousness, awakes in us the strongest aspirations for good of which our poor nature is capable, this will remain a singularly unsympathetic and shortsighted pronouncement. Our Lord certainly set aside much that entered into the hopes and aspirations of his followers, and taught them much that seemed to give the lie to their most sacred convictions. But in doing so he was interpreting to them what their own prophets had taught,—the inmost secret of the hope they had faithfully in their ignorance kept alive, and to that hope he assured the future of the world.

[1] Goldwin Smith, *Guesses at the Riddle of Existence* (1897), p. 117 f.

This is the end of this publication.

Any remaining blank pages are for our book binding
requirements and are blank on purpose.

To search thousands of interesting publications like this one,
please remember to visit our website at:

http://www.kessinger.net

CPSIA information can be obtained at www.ICGtesting.com
Printed in the USA
LVOW04s2002190215

427563LV00021B/576/P